Growing Roses

Everything You Need to Know
....and More

By Susan Sumner

www.WhentoPlantRoses.com

Growing Roses
Everything You Need to Know and More . . .
Author: Susan Sumner
© Blurtigo Holdings, LLC
2nd Edition

First Printing 2012 – Printed in United States of America

Disclaimer and Terms of Use: The Author and Publisher have strived to be as accurate and complete as possible in the creation of this book. While all attempts have been made to verify information provided in this publication, the Author and Publisher assume no responsibility for errors, omissions, or contrary interpretation of the subject matter herein. Any perceived slights of specific persons, peoples, or organizations are unintentional. In practical advice books, like anything else in life, there are no guarantees of outcomes resulting from information in this book.

This book is dedicated to Bella
Like the rose, you are a beauty in every way!
Thank you for being one of the great joys of my life

...for buying my book!
If you like it, please be kind and
review on Amazon.com.

Susan Sumner

Visit my Author's Page at
http://www.amazon.com/author/susansumner

Growing Roses

Table of Contents

Growing Roses

Preface

Whether you are enjoying the rich fragrance and glorious colors of three long-stem rosebuds freshly cut from your garden as you quietly sip your first cup of coffee, or are joyfully accepting the surprise gift of a single rose from someone you love, a rose is always met with a smile and a sweet softness in the heart. It symbolizes everything that is beautiful in life.

The rose is the most beloved flower of all time! It is intricately intertwined with the mystique of love and romance. It captures the essence and allure of love -- young love, mature love, and perhaps even the love of life! No other flower creates such a profound response in so many people of all ages. Is it any wonder that it is so popular?

Flowers are a great addition to any garden, and/or room's decor. They add color, fragrance, and elegance in spaces that may otherwise be drab and boring. Nothing can offer quite as much instant beauty as a great floral arrangement, especially if those flowers are roses.

For centuries, roses have come to characterize great taste and eternity during events such as weddings, anniversaries, and birthdays. They are always the flower of choice when someone is hoping to create a bond with another.

Anyone can purchase roses in a gift shop or florist, but it takes a special person to want to grow their own roses. In spite of all their beauty, there is a belief by some that these incredible flowers are difficult to handle . . . and I am not talking about the thorns. They have the reputation of being difficult task masters.

There may be a bit of truth to those rumors if your goal is to become a national champion with your award-winning roses, which BTW will require above and beyond care. But, for you, me and everyone who simply wants to enjoy them in our own little garden for personal delight, the rumors are untrue. Growing roses may require a little more care than other flowers, but not much. They are definitely not the "mighty monsters" that many people claim.

If you are new to the world of growing roses, this book provides a nice introduction with an overview of roses and their varieties, as well as step-by-step tips to help you care for your new amazing plants.

By the time you have finished reading this, you will be prepared to add the beauty of roses to your garden.

How to Use the Book

My goal for the book is to help you as much as possible with this delightful new adventure. There is a lot to absorb in one reading, so relax and enjoy it. Note the sections that you know you will want to read again for better understanding.

At first glance, you may feel a bit overwhelmed by all of the things that you need to know before you can begin to plant your roses, but that will soon disappear after you read all of the easy to follow instructions outlined in this guide.

The information will help you choose the types of roses that suit your personal tastes and personality; it will help you understand which roses will do well with the climatic conditions of your area, and give you direction on the when and how to plant your roses to make sure they survive whatever Mother Nature throws at them - the freezing cold or the blazing summer heat. We can't control Mother Nature, but we can protect the roses from her wrath most of the time.

At the end of the book, there is a glossary to help you "learn the language" of rosarians. It is great fun to "talk the talk" with others, who love, grow and care for one of the oldest and most beautiful flower families in the world – the rose!

Types of Roses

Let's begin at the beginning by introducing you to the types of roses. As you read through the following information, don't be stressed by all the different types, your choices will be easier than you think. Simply choose the ones that appeal to you, keeping in mind the primary reason you have decided to plant roses.

One of the most common ways that the roses are grouped is through the date of introduction.

ROSES	DESCRIPTION
Species Roses	These have been growing in the wild for hundreds, if not thousands, of years
Old Garden Roses	Introduced prior to 1867, which was the year the hybrid tea rose 'La France' was introduced
Modern Roses	Roses introduced in 1867 or later

Roses are divided by sub-categories within their larger classifications, usually identified by their physical characteristics, such as their growing habits, foliage traits, or even their flower forms.

The modern rose category is the one that is readily available, so let's take a look at the basic differences of each type.

Modern Roses	Description
Hybrid Tea	Upright plant; tall, high centered; blooms continually throughout the season; long stemmed; generally one bloom per stem; classic rose used for cut flowers; not usually good for the novice grower
Floribunda	Compact bush hardier than hybrid teas; blooms continually throughout season; fragrant, smaller blooms that hybrid teas; grow in clusters on short stems; good for cutting; beautiful combination of hybrid tea and polyanthus
Grandiflora	Upright plants; high centered; single or in clusters on tall plants; stems long enough for cutting; lots of colorful blooms
Polyantha	Compact, hardy, can grow quite large (height and width); generous small blooms in large clusters
Shrub	Large plants; hardy and easy to grow; great for landscaping; many color choices; bloom continually throughout season; disease resistant; require less maintenance.
Miniatures	Smaller versions of larger modern roses; bush sizes range from 6 inches to 6 feet (most commonly 1 to 2 feet); leaves and flowers in perfect proportion; great color for small spaces; good for cold climates; also good indoors in pots
Climbers	Mixed group; long, arching canes in need of support; can be trained to grow vertically or horizontally like vines on trellises, arches, or walls; some bloom only in the spring, others throughout season; group includes climbing hybrid tea, climbing floribunda, climbing grandiflora, hybrid wichurana, large-flowered climber, climbing miniature classes
Knockout Roses	Latest entry into the rose family; easy to grow shrub 3' X 3', clusters of 3-inch flowers; light and delicate fragrance; bloom throughout the season; not good for cutting

Choosing the Right Roses

You may be tempted to just run to the closest nursery or home-gardening center and pick the most beautiful rose plant you see; but, I encourage you to put more thought into it than that. After all, you will be investing both your time and money into this project – and you want it to be successful. A little research would be wise.

To help you make the best choice for your garden, consider the following:

- Why have you decided to plant roses: Do you want season-long color; do you want a sprawling plant that will cover a large area; do you want to fill a small space with color; do you want long-stemmed roses that can be cut frequently for inside enjoyment, etc? This is an important point that should be clear before you begin your decision-making process.

- Color may seem like a trivial matter, but not if you have a personal preference for specific colors. Since there are so many choices, pick colors that are personally appealing.

- If certain fragrances invoke an allergic reaction for you or any member of your family, you will want to plant roses that have a softer fragrance.

- Rose plants come in all sizes! The final growth height of a rose bush should be considered carefully. What is the size of the space that you want to fill – height and width? Do you want a large climbing plant than can grow up to 30 feet? Or are you looking for a smaller, more delicate version of a climber to grace the small arbor in your garden?

- How much time do you have to invest in the flowers? If you have the time and energy to get intimately involved with the plant, hybrid tea roses are a good choice, but they require regular pruning and are prone to disease; but, there are other equally beautiful choices that are much hardier and require less maintenance.

- What is the climate of your area? If you have very cold winters, you want a rose that will survive during the off season. If you have very hot summers, you must choose a rose that will withstand the heat during the blooming season. I recommend that you check the **USDA Plant Hardiness Zone Map**, which will help you make a good decision about the type of rose that will thrive in your climate.

- After you have narrowed your choices down to two or three, go deeper with your investigation. Talk to your nurseryman or research online. Study the pros and cons of choosing one type of rose over another.

- If you are hoping to cut your roses for display inside your home or use in creating bouquets, you must choose a type that is compatible with this purpose. Hybrid teas are a good choice. Be aware that some roses will fall apart at the petals if they are cut.

- Consider what *other* types of flowers or plants are in your garden, or that you intend to add to your garden. You want to add plants and flowers that will not create a damaging environment to your rose's ecosystem.

Planting Roses

Planting roses does not have to be difficult. With some basic knowledge and key steps for planting, you can plant and nurture a single rosebush or create a magnificent rose garden.

Helpful Tips for Planting your Roses

- Check with your local gardening center for the best type of roses to grow in your climate.

- If you are a novice, you should look for disease resistant types of roses because they require less maintenance.

- Spring planting is the best.

- Most roses require at least six hours of good sunlight daily (morning sun is best). Adequate sunlight is a key to growing beautiful roses. Even those that are considered shade compatible will need a minimum of four hours. Some climbing roses will thrive in partial shade. *DO NOT knock your head against that brick wall by filling a shaded space with a rose plant that needs sun.*

- There must also be good air circulation around your roses. They will not grow well in an enclosed or tight area.

- The soil must be well-drained. Roses do not like soggy soil. Don't plant where water tends to stand idle after a rain. If you don't have a good well-drained area, one solution is to build a raised flower bed.

- Check the PH level of the soil. This is the single most important element in the soil. The ideal amount of acid in the soil is 6 to 6.5 but roses can do well with a range of 5.6 to 7.2. You can get a testing kit for your soil at any garden center. It is much easier to take care of this before you plant than to try to correct after you plant.

- Clear any existing vegetation from the site you have chosen, dig and turn the soil at least two feet deep. For every three buckets of soil add one bucket of organic material (compost or manure) to improve the nutrient content in the soil.

- Dig a proper hole – two feet across and two feet deep for each plant. This provides adequate space for the root system to reach and grow properly. If the hole is too small, fungal infections are more likely.

- Get specific instructions from the nursery on how to prepare the rose bush and the hole for planting. These instructions will vary depending on whether the plant is barefoot or container-grown.

- During the first 3-4 weeks after planting your roses, you should water them often. Deep watering helps the roots push deep into the soil, which will allow them to do better in long-hot dry seasons. Roses need a lot of hydration and food to remain healthy.

- Four weeks after planting, you should start soaking the bed regularly – every week or two. You should do this in the morning for the best results. Check with your local nursery regarding the best watering schedule for your climate.

- Begin fertilization approximately three months after planting. Try to stick with organic materials as much as possible. Use 3-6 inches of mulch to control the moisture, temperature, and weed growth. Mulch also helps to lock in the vital nutrients your roses need to remain healthy.

Watering Roses

Watering your roses can be a tricky thing. It is one of the most important aspects of taking care of your roses. Roses need almost as much water to stay healthy as people do. Of course there are quite a few things that must be considered before you water your roses.

Points to Remember

- Roses love water, but they hate standing in pools of water. Be sure that the area around them drains well.

- On average they require approximately one to two inches of water every week – and even more in hotter, very dry periods. Good rule of thumb is to water your plants two to four times a week for approximately 30 minutes a session.

- Be sure to water in the early morning so that the leaves have time to dry before nightfall. If leaves don't dry before the sun goes down, they may develop a fungal disease.

- Periodically check the depth to which the water is penetrating. Make sure the moisture is reaching the complete root system. You would be surprised how large the root system area is – especially for larger, established roses. The root system could be as deep as a foot or a foot and a half.

- You will learn quickly enough how much water your plant needs. Part of it depends on the type of soil you have – sandy soil needs more frequent watering than heavier clay soils.

- If you are over-watering, the leaves will turn yellow and may eventually drop off. If you are under-watering, the leaves will go limp and sag.

- You may want to give the plants a shower once a week. This provides the plant with much needed humidity and cleans dust, dirt, and even spider mites off the leaves. BUT – this *must be done in the early morning* so they are completely dry before nightfall.

- To help you lower the risk of your roses getting diseases, mulch is a nice way to keep the soil moist, without allowing all of the fungal problems that too much moisture can cause. Mulch also helps deter the growth of weeds around the plant.

- Good choices for mulch are: wood chips and stray or dry grass clippings. Apply the mulch two to three inches deep. Decomposition of mulch can strip the soil of nutrients so fertilizer will be necessary.

Fertilizing Roses

A good fertilizing program is more than just a bunch of . . . well, you get the idea. Fertilizing is the way you ensure that your roses receive their share of nourishment to keep them looking beautiful for years to come.

If you decide to use mulch to protect your plant in other ways, you must use fertilizer; but, fertilizing your plant is a good idea whether you use mulch or not.

Be careful using chemical fertilizers, herbicides, and pesticides because they destroy natural soil organisms and disrupt the natural relationship between the roses and the soil. Without helpful bacteria to protect the roots, harmful fungi develop and harm the plant.

The rose plants also become addicted to chemical fertilizers to the point that they will not bloom well without them. The more you use the chemicals, the more the roses depend on them. Organic fertilizers are always the best first choice.

General Guidelines for Fertilizing

- Species roses only need annual spring fertilization.

- All others – fertilize in the spring and add a second application around mid-June or towards the end of the spring blooming period.

- If you have any repeat-bloomers, consider a third application of fertilizer – in the middle of July.

- Whatever you do – do not apply any fertilizer after mid-August. You don't want to encourage growth that could be damaged by the upcoming winter months.

- You should never fertilize plants that are heat or water stressed. Water-stressed plants that grow under a lot of heat will suffer leaf and bud burn.

- Fertilize when there is a steady air temperature of approximately 70-80 degrees so that your plants will absorb the most nutrients possible.

- For best results when you spread fertilizer, there is an optimum approach you can use:

    o Spread the fertilizer out in a circular band around the plant, about half a foot from its crown. Make the width of the applied fertilizer about 18 inches wide. Work the fertilizer in lightly, then water it. This ensures that the fertilizer gets down to the root system.

- If time is a problem and you cannot keep up with the feeding schedule, there is a good time-release fertilizer called Osmocote fertilizer. It is composed of dry, encapsulated nutrients that are released slowly throughout the growing season. They are released in four-, six-, or even eight-month intervals, depending on the formula. Osmocote should be applied in May (one-half cup per plant).

Pruning Roses

Regular pruning is critical for most roses (except the climbers, which need pruning less often). Some rose growers feel this is a necessary annoyance, but I happen to enjoy it. It takes a steady hand and the proper procedure to ensure that you have the most beautiful roses possible.

Pruning removes all the dead and damaged pieces of the plant, and teaches the new growth to grow in the correct outward facing direction. Proper pruning also aids in the proper circulation of air to ensure that your roses remain healthy.

Techniques to Guide You Through the Pruning Process

- Prune in the early spring, just after the snow melts or the temperatures begin to warm in more temperate climates. This will help protect your roses from disease and insects.

- Hand shears are the best tool for pruning the smaller branches. Loppers are best for the thicker branches (thickness of a pencil). Protect your hands from the thorns with a heavy pair of rose gloves.

- Use *bypass pruning shears* that work like scissors and *not the anvil types* because the anvils crush the stems and make the roses more susceptible to diseases.

- Always sharpen your hand shears before pruning. Even though climbers only have to be pruned every couple of years, prune them with caution. The branches have a tendency to overlap and you wouldn't want to prune the wrong branches.

- Soak your pruning shears in equal parts of water and bleach. This will help to protect your roses from diseases and insects.

- You want to get rid of the dead wood first. (That would be the black wood that is black inside as well as out).

- Next, prune out any stems that are thinner than a pencil. You should cut all but five of the leftover healthy branches, which are often dark green and about the thickness of a pencil.

- Cut all of the branches that cross or overlap one another because these are often diseased or will become so.

- You will want to make your rose bush fluted or vase-shaped, with an open center, with no overlapping or touching stems. Cut so that the bud is facing outside of the bush and at a 45 degree angle that slopes inward so that you can keep promoting the outward growth.

- Cut the bushes by approximately one third or one half, depending on how tall you want them. Cut your healthy canes to be about one to four feet long, or whatever size that you prefer.

- Cut above the outward facing buds, which are the buds that are on the outside of the rosebush. This will help the bud to grow upward, allowing the center of the bud to open up for better air circulation and shape.

Caring for Roses

Roses have the reputation of being difficult to care for, but in reality, that is not completely true. If you have chosen carefully and selected a type that accommodates to your climate, and take care with the planting process, your problems will be at a minimum.

There are many small things that have to be done to keep your roses looking their best. Create a simple schedule of what needs to be done (and when), follow it religiously, and soon it will become part of your regular routine.

Great Tips for the Regular Upkeep of Your Roses

- Be sure you cover the "trinity of care" – fertilizing, watering, and grooming. Roses love to eat and must have the proper nutrients; they need a good water supply on a regular schedule; and they have to be groomed. (See detailed instructions for each in previous sections.)

- Mulching is important because it helps to keep your maintenance down a bit. Mulching requires your roses to need a lot less watering, weeding and helps prevent diseases. The best mulches are organic ones like wood chips, pine needles, and grass clippings.

- Keep the area around your roses cleared to prevent them from getting locked in an area that doesn't provide enough circulation.

- Learn about and take the necessary steps to protect your plants from disease and pest infestation.

- Protect your roses during the winter months – prepare them for the cold. There are at least two good ways that will work for most rose plants:

    1. Create a makeshift parka for your plants by heaping the base of the roses with compost and manure in the late fall or early winter prior to the brunt of the cold weather.

    2. Don't prune back the roses in the fall. This provides sacrificial growth that catches the frost and protects the core plant. These should provide the necessary protection from the winter weather.

- Avoid the white plastic cones when doing your winter protection because they trap too much heat during the winter thaw. They are also quite unattractive.

Preventing Common Rose Diseases

Roses are susceptible to diseases; some types are more susceptible than others. Many of the problems that come with having roses are relatively easy to take care of, but it is always better to stop them all together rather than having to cure them later.

Steps to Prevent Diseases from Reaching Your Roses

- If you want to avoid disease problems as much as possible, buy roses that are more disease resistant and low maintenance like shrubs and landscape roses.

- Planting your roses properly in areas that have a lot of sun (at least 6 hours in the morning), with adequate air circulation and good compost for faster draining can prevent many problems later.

- Keeping different types of flowers and plants in with your roses will help to provide your roses with a better and more balanced ecosystem surrounding it.

- Fertilize your plants in the proper manner. Roses need their food too! (See section on fertilizing for the best methods.)

- Watering your roses in early morning hours will help to keep fungal diseases from hitting your roses. (See section on watering for the best techniques.)

- A two-inch layer (minimum) of mulch at the base of your roses will help keep soil born diseases at bay.

- Watch for any indication of disease or pest problems and take care of the issues immediately. Wishing it weren't so will not make the problems go away.

Handling Disease and Pest Problems

No matter how hard you try and even with the best prevention techniques in place, you will not always be able to stop disease and pest infestation from affecting your roses. Don't worry, there are solutions! All it takes is a little bit of tender loving care, and the right techniques.

Important Tips to Remember

- Act early and act often. Catch the problem in the early stages and it will be easy to resolve.

- The best line of defense is always the natural approach. If you don't have to resort to chemicals, don't!

- Roses attract aphids and beetles. Aphids are the biggest problem you will face.

- First step: If you see aphids, knock them off with squirts of water. Be sure to rinse off the underside of the rose foliage to remove any mites hidden from view. Clean foliage is healthy foliage.

- If that doesn't work, there are several good pesticides that can take care of aphids very quickly.

- If you prefer organic solutions, look for insecticidal soaps that can be found at your local nursery or a home improvement store.

- Beetles – the most common is the Japanese beetle. They will quickly destroy a bloom. If you see a beetle, it is too late to save the bloom. Some experts advise using Malathion, Diazinon, or other insecticides as soon as you seen the beetle and continue to apply the formula on a regular basis.

- The organic solution for beetles is to plant garlic plants near your roses and the beetles will stay away. You can also find a garlic spray that will have the same effect.

- Roses are particularly susceptible to three types of diseases: Black Spot, Powdery and Downy Mildews, and Rose Rust. Each of these is a fungus infection and each can be treated with fungicide. The main thing is DO NOT WAIT! At the very first sign of disease, apply the fungicide. As part of the treatment – always remove all dead and seriously infested leaves and stems.

- You may even want to take preventative measures by applying the fungicide if you know that hot and humid weather is approaching.

- A good home remedy for powder mildew is to make a mixture of 1 gallon of water; 2 TBSP of baking soda; 1 TBSP of Murphy's Oil Soap and spray over the roses in the morning every two weeks until the overall temperature around the roses reaches 80 degrees.

- Midge are tiny maggots that causes the rose's buds to blacken from the damage. If you want to fix this problem, prune the affected area and then destroy it.

Growing Roses Organically

Many people are now getting into growing all things organic. Farmers are doing it with produce and meats, so it is natural that you may want to grow your roses that way also. Many people have problems using the pesticides and insecticides that go along with growing roses and keeping them healthy. There are more natural methods of growing your roses.

Step-by-step Method for Growing Roses Organically

- Each bush that you want to plant will need a foot of space all around it so that the flowers can get the proper amount of circulation, which helps to prevent leaf diseases.

- Purchase organic roses. Look for roses that have a sturdy green stem and no blemishes on them. Bare root roses are best for this.

- Along with roses that have green stems, look for stems that have evenly spaced leaves that are close together.

- Be sure the soil is well drained. This promotes healthy growth because the plant will have all the water and nutrients it needs from the root to the flower's head. Build a raised bed if drainage is a constant problem.

- Ask your local garden center about the best approach to ensure organically correct soil.

- Soak your bare root roses in a large container of compost tea for many hours before you plant them.

- Plant the rose at the point where the stem breaks into the root so that it is at soil level, or approximately one inch below the top level if you live in an area that is prone to hard winters.

- Check the bare root roses carefully. If your roots grow out in a tight circle, you have to cut a straight slice down each of its four sides. A knife is good for this. Then you will dig a hole that is two inches deeper than the container and at least twice as wide.

- Mix your organic garden soil with an equal amount of compost and use your hands to gently spread the roots into the soil mix.

- Mulch to help prevent your roses from being exposed to weeds, and water stress complications. It will also ensure that your roses remain at their lowest possible maintenance level.

- Feed your roses organically also. Fertilize with organic fertilizer and maintain a regular watering schedule.

- Water your organic roses deep at the planting, and then once every week after that during growing season so that you can promote deep roots. Watering in the early morning is best.

- Cultivate the top inch of your soil around each of your roses and fertilize on a monthly basis with a balanced organic fertilizer. Use a good granular type of fertilizer that you can work into the soil. Either that, or you can use a fish emulsion or seaweed based product that you can mix with water because it has all of the necessary nutrients that a healthy flower needs. Check the ingredients listed on the labels to ensure that they have nitrogen, phosphorus, potassium, iron and calcium.

- To help protect your bed against the various types of pests and insects that can plague your roses, put sticky yellow bars every ten feet to catch them.

- You may use an organic pesticide if the problem is bad.

- If your pest problem is severe enough, you may use insecticidal soap to spray over your roses.

Now you have all of the necessary knowledge that you need to grow your own bed of earth friendly roses. Your flowers will be just as beautiful as those that are not grown organically, and will likely have the healthiest life span that a rose can get. Organic roses have some of the best color and "immune systems" that roses can have. The fragrance of them cannot be beaten.

Boosting Your Roses in the Spring

Every spring people get a boost of energy. It is like the very air in the spring time is rejuvenating in itself. Natural passions and new loves are often born in the spring, and old loves get a nice spark between them. Spring is definitely the best time of year.

The same goes for roses. It is in the spring that people beginning planting or replenishing their rose gardens. For those bushes that are already established, spring is the time to see new buds beginning to appear.

You may want to try this special tonic that is used to give your roses a strong boost of nutrients they need in order for them to remain strong and healthy and to produce many blooms throughout the season.

Mix the following ingredients in a 5-gallon tub or bucket:

> 2 cups of alfalfa meal
> 2 cups of Epsom salt
> 2 cups of fish meal
> 2 cups of gypsum
> 2 cups of greensand
> 1 cup of bone meal

- Apply in the early spring after you have removed any of the necessary winter protection that you may have had in place.

- Pull back the mulch that has been placed around the plants.

- Work one cup of the tonic into the top one inch of soil for smaller bushes.

- Use a trowel or a hand cultivator for larger bushes (bushes six feet or taller). The taller bushes will need three or four cups.

- Replace the mulch and water your roses very well.

Extra Tip #1: You can do this again in the middle of June if you want to keep your roses blooming. Just gently scratch two cups of the mixture into the soil.

Extra Tip #2: You should wear a dust mask while you are mixing your ingredients for the tonic.

Drying Roses

There are many reasons why you may want to dry your roses. Some people just want to keep a memento of a special moment. Perhaps they are a part of a wedding that you went to; maybe they were a gift from a lover, friend, or family member. Whatever your reasons for doing it, this is the section where you will learn to dry your roses properly.

There two ways to dry your roses that are inexpensive and relatively easy.

Air Drying – The Easiest and Least Expensive

- Start with perfect and unflawed roses on their stems. If the roses are not in perfect condition, they will wither and the petals will fall off.

- Remove any leaves that may be on the branches.

- Bunch them up together in a manner that lets them fan out.

- Tie the bottom with string or a rubber band.

- Hang them upside down in a dark, dry place for two to three weeks to be certain that they are completely dry.

Sand Drying

- Start by picking the roses that are in perfect condition. They shouldn't have any dew on them and the stems should be dry as well.

- Reinforce the stems and blossom with either white glue or florist wire.

- For florist wire, you will want to cut off most of the stem. Leave about one inch of stem.

- Push about three inches of wire through the stem and right through the flower head.

- Bend the end of the wire into a hook over each rose head and pull it down. This helps to keep the head secured to the stem.

- When choosing to use the glue, begin by diluting the glue in a dab of water.

- Take a toothpick and dab a thin coat of the glue mixture at the base of each petal.

- Work the glue into the base of the stems of each flower so that you can attach each petal to the base. Then, wait until the glue dries completely

- Now for the sand, slowly and carefully cover the flowers with sand in deep open boxes.

- Make the sand in the box deep enough to hold the flowers upright.

- Set each flower in the sand filled box and slowly pour sand around the base, around the sides, and over and under the petals. You should pour the sand evenly so that you can preserve the flowers' natural shape.

- Wait for the flowers to dry while facing upright.

- Put the boxes with the roses in a dry space that is warm and brightly lit. This will ensure that your roses will maintain their bright color.

- Let them dry for one to three weeks.

- If you want more muted colors, you will want to dry them in a more humid area.

- To remove the sand, tip the drying container slightly so that the sand can fall off the flowers.

- Remove each flower one by one.

Dried flowers will make great decorations for any room in your house or office, or great gifts to friends and family members.

Growing Roses

Selecting Cold Climate Roses

Most roses will grow just about anywhere, and in any type of climate. However, there are a few that simply do not function well in cold climates; for example, Hybrid Tea Roses do not do well with cold weather. They must be grown in a warmer climate like Florida. They simply don't have the necessary winter protection that is required to survive the winter weather.

If you live in an area that is prone to harsh winters, check with your local garden center to find out which rose plants will thrive in your area. Otherwise, you will be wasting your time and money by planting roses that cannot survive in cold climates.

Although the choices are somewhat limited, cold climate roses are wonderful for several reasons. They are very low maintenance flowers, which is especially good for the novice. Cold climate roses are very hardy and have built-in protection against diseases and bacteria that can plague other types of roses.

Below is a short list of the ones I would recommend. Of course there are more, but this is a good start.

Cold Climate Roses

Rugosas	Species Roses
Griffith Buck	Gallica
Modern Roses	Alba
Centrifolias	Shrub Roses

No matter where you live, you can enjoy the beauty of roses in your garden.

~BONUS~
Reviving Wilted Cut Roses

Roses add elegance that is unsurpassed by any other flower wherever they are placed.

As beautiful as roses are, they do have a certain vulnerability that is common to any cut flower. They are prone to sag, droop and wilt after a few days in a vase. Everyone would like to preserve that beauty for as long as possible, and I have a secret that will help save your roses when this happens to you.

- Remove the roses from the vase.

- Separate the roses, but keep them submerged in lukewarm water as you do it.

- Make a fresh cut on the stem, again while it remains in the water because you don't want to expose the stem to air.

- Take each flower, one by one and roll them in newspaper and close the paper with a rubber band to keep it from unrolling.

- Put each rose while still wrapped in the newspaper in a sink or tub filled with water and let them soak for several hours while still separate.

- Once they have soaked, unwrap them carefully, and place them in a vase of fresh warm water.

- If you want to preserve the health of your roses, put some 7UP® in the water to help prevent any bacteria that can clog up the stem.

Extra tip: Roses droop for one of two reasons. Either they had been cut too early when put into the vase, or they may have been out of water too long before putting them into the vase.

Conclusion

If this book has furthered your knowledge about growing roses, fueled your love for them, and helped to established even one plant in your garden, it has been well worth the time and energy I put into writing it.

This may be the first book you have bought on growing roses, but I am hoping it won't be your last.

Enjoy your new adventure and the thrill of seeing that first amazing bud begin to open. Watch them grow in your garden, enjoy the sweet fragrances, and bask in their beauty as you grace your home with a single rose or a full bouquet.

Enjoy the experience!

Susan Sumner

www.WhentoPlantRoses.com

References

The American Rose Society. www.ars.org

Belendez, K. *Grandma's mason jar*. Retrieved 15 Jun 09 from
http://scvrs.homestead.com/Cuttings1.html.

Better Homes and Gardens. *Protect roses from pests & diseases.*
Retrieved 14 Jun 09 from
http://www.bhg.com/gardening/flowers/roses/protect-
roses-from-pests-diseases/, accessed 14 Jun 09

Climate Zones for Roses, What Are They? Retrieved 14 Jun 09
from http://www.ars.org/About_Roses/climate_zones-
whatarethey.html.

GardenStewBlog. *How to transplant roses and prune roses.*
Retrieved 14 Jun 09 from
http://www.gardenstew.com/blog/e283-86-how-to-
transplant-and-prune-roses-graphic-heavy.html.

Garden-Web. http://forums.gardenweb.com/forums

HelpMeFind. Retrieved 15 Jun 09 from
www.helpmefind.com/roses

Iannotti, M. *Growing miniature roses.* Retrieved 17 Jun 09 from
http://gardening.about.com/od/rose1/a/MiniRose.htm

Ondra, N. J. (2001). *Taylor's Guide to Roses.* Houghton-Mifflin
Publishing, NYC, NY.

Owen, D. *Raising Roses and Your Climate Zone.* Retrieve 14 Jun 09 from http://ezinearticles.com/?Raising-Roses-and-Your-Climate-Zone&id=493622.

Patton, D. *Watering roses.* Retrieved 15 Jun 09 from http://extension.missouri.edu/extensioninfonet/article.asp?id=1504.

Watering Roses. *Roses love water.* Retrieved 7 April 2012 from http://www.rose.org/watering-roses/.

Growing Roses

Appendix I
Glossary of Terms

Below is a quick-reference glossary of many (but by no means all) of the terms you may encounter as you continue on with your love affair with roses.

Term	Definition
Anther	The upper portion of the stamen; contains the pollen sacs
Apical Meristem	Cells which did not mature at the tip of shoots and roots producing the hormone auxin
Auricle	The "earlike" project on the tip of the stipule
Auxin	The hormone regulating the bloom cycle
Axil	Angle on upper side where the leaf joins the stem
Axillary	Any bud or branch in the axil of a leaf; these grow following pruning
Bark	Outer layer of the cane of a rose
Bract	A leaf that is usually smaller or shaped differently than others on the plant; grows under the peduncle just below the flower
Bud	Embryonic shoot that will produce either flowers or foliage
Bud union	Area between the roots and stems where the bud of a different plant has been grafted onto the rootstock
Calyx	A series of flower parts which grow from the peduncle; made of sepals, usually green and leaf-like that protect the flower bud
Cane	Stem of the rose -- either the main stem (sometimes called the trunk) or lateral stems and branches
Carpel	An organ which holds the ovules along its margins; part of the compound pistil
Compound leaf	Leaf made of two or more parts or leaflets

Corolla	Second series of flower parts growing from the peduncle; composed of petal
Double	Refers to the number of petals on a bloom, normally agreed to being between 25 and 45.
Filament	Stalk of the stamen supporting the anther
Floral tube	Cup-like structure formed by fusion of the basal parts of the sepals, petals, and stamens.
Fruit	Ripe ovary containing seeds and any adjacent parts
Hip	Fruit of the rose containing the seeds
Leaf	Organ that arises laterally from a shoot apex. Usually flat; may be simple or compound
Leaf scar	Mark left on the stem when the leaf detaches; above each of these is a bud
Meristem	Tissue made of cells that do not mature, but remain capable of growing and dividing; present in growing tips
Mixed buds	Buds that produce both leaves and flowers; usual type of bud on rose; present in leaf axils
Ovary	Swollen basal portion of the pistil containing the ovules or the seeds
Ovule	Structure containing the embryo sac, nucellus, integuments and stalk. Following fertilization this develops into seeds
Peduncle	Main cane of a spray or an individual flower
Pedicel	Stem of an individual flower in a spray
Perianth	Collective term for the calyx and corolla (sepals and petals) combined
Petal	One of the units of the corolla of a flower. Roses have from four to more than 100 petals, depending on the variety
Petiole	Stalk of the leaf
Petiolul	Subdivision of petiole connecting the lateral leaflets to the petiole
Pistil	Central organ of the flower made of one or more carpels; enclosing the ovule

Pith	Soft inner portion of stem
Pollen	Granules within pollen sacs which contain genetic information used for sexual reproduction
Prickle	Spine-like superficial outgrowth of the stem; roses technically have prickles, not thorns
Roots	Underground portions of the rose used for support, and absorption and delivery of water and nutrients
Rootstock	Cultivated roots implanted with a bud of another variety; sometimes called grafting
Semi-double	Refers to number of petals on bloom -- usually 12 to 25 in this category
Sepal	One unit of calyx; green coverings of a flower bud which open to reveal petals; roses normally have five sepals
Single	Refers to number of petals the bloom has -- customarily four to eight
Spray	Several flowers' buds arising from one peduncle; develop into many flowers on short pedicels
Stamen	Organ of flower producing pollen, made of anther and filament
Stigma	Top of pistil, the section that receives the pollen grains
Stipule	Leaf appendage usually present in roses on the petiole where it meets the stem
Style	Portion of the pistil connecting ovary and stigma
Terminal	Buds at the end of branches
Thorn	Branch of a plant that becomes woody, hard, and pointed; not to be confused with prickles
Trunk	Main stem; the cane that eventually produces all the side branches or lateral canes

Made in the USA
Columbia, SC
13 September 2021

45441081R00033